TRUMP:

★ THE ART OF THE PRESIDENCY ★

D.A. DENNISON

w
White Road Press

Copyright © 2018 by White Road Press LLC / We're Better Than This

All rights reserved. Printed in the United States of America.
Published by White Road Press.

No part of this book may be used or reproduced in any manner whatsoever without written permission except in the case of brief quotations embodied in critical articles and reviews.

Cover design by Mondelux

Library of Congress Cataloging-in-Publication Data has been applied for.

ISBN: 978-1-642-54449-7

Core Belief #1:

Trump: The Art of the Presidency

Trump: The Art of the Presidency

Trump: The Art of the Presidency

Trump: The Art of the Presidency

Core Belief #2:

Trump: The Art of the Presidency

Trump: The Art of the Presidency

Trump: The Art of the Presidency

Trump: The Art of the Presidency

Core Belief #3:

Trump: The Art of the Presidency

Trump: The Art of the Presidency

Trump: The Art of the Presidency

Trump: The Art of the Presidency

Core Belief #4:

Trump: The Art of the Presidency

Trump: The Art of the Presidency

Trump: The Art of the Presidency

Trump: The Art of the Presidency

Core Belief #5:

Trump: The Art of the Presidency

Trump: The Art of the Presidency

Trump: The Art of the Presidency

Trump: The Art of the Presidency

Core Belief #6:

Trump: The Art of the Presidency

Trump: The Art of the Presidency

Trump: The Art of the Presidency

Trump: The Art of the Presidency

Core Belief #7:

Trump: The Art of the Presidency

Trump: The Art of the Presidency

Trump: The Art of the Presidency

Trump: The Art of the Presidency

Core Belief #8:

Trump: The Art of the Presidency

Trump: The Art of the Presidency

Trump: The Art of the Presidency

Trump: The Art of the Presidency

Core Belief #9:

Trump: The Art of the Presidency

Trump: The Art of the Presidency

Trump: The Art of the Presidency

Trump: The Art of the Presidency

Core Belief #10:

Trump: The Art of the Presidency

Trump: The Art of the Presidency

Trump: The Art of the Presidency

Trump: The Art of the Presidency

Core Belief #11:

Trump: The Art of the Presidency

Trump: The Art of the Presidency

Trump: The Art of the Presidency

Trump: The Art of the Presidency

Core Belief #12:

Trump: The Art of the Presidency

Trump: The Art of the Presidency

Trump: The Art of the Presidency

Trump: The Art of the Presidency

Trump: The Art of the Presidency

Trump: The Art of the Presidency

Trump: The Art of the Presidency

Made in the USA
Columbia, SC
08 October 2018